THE BRONTË SISTERS

from a painting of about 1835 by PATRICK BRANWELL BRONTË
National Portrait Gallery

Anne on the left   Emily in the centre   Charlotte on the right

THE BRONTË SISTERS

by

PHYLLIS BENTLEY

PUBLISHED FOR
THE BRITISH COUNCIL
BY LONGMAN GROUP LTD

LONGMAN GROUP LTD
Longman House, Burnt Mill, Harlow, Essex

*Associated companies, branches and
representatives throughout the world*

*First published 1950
Revised editions 1954, 1959, 1963
Reprinted with minor corrections to text and additions to
Bibliography 1967, 1971*
© Phyllis Bentley, 1959, 1963, 1971

*Printed in Great Britain by
F. Mildner & Sons, London, EC1R 5EJ*

SBN 0 582 01004 7

THE BRONTË SISTERS

I. INTRODUCTION

THE Brontë sisters form a curious and interesting phenomenon in English literature, in that during the hundred years since their death not only has critical appreciation of their work continually heightened, but also what amounts to a popular cult has grown about their name. The number of works of criticism on the Brontë writings is only exceeded, I believe, by those on Shakespeare, while statistics from libraries and publishers reveal that when the great English novelists of the past are placed in order of present reading popularity, the Brontës veer between second and third place. During the last two decades many plays, novels, and films, of varying type and accuracy, have been founded on their fictions and their lives. The Brontë Society, established in 1893 for the preservation of Brontë relics and study of Brontë works, flourishes strongly and publishes yearly *Transactions* containing fresh pieces of Brontë research. Most striking facts, perhaps, of all: in 1947, centenary of the first publication of Brontë fiction, more than fifty thousand persons visited the not very easily accessible Haworth Parsonage, now a Brontë Museum; by 1969 attendances had risen to over one hundred and six thousand.

Nor is this cult confined to England. The extent of Brontë reading and study conducted in other languages is quite remarkable. I myself receive correspondence on Brontë subjects from many diverse nations, including France, the United States and Japan. The Brontës seem to appeal alike to the student of literature, the poet, the mystic, the moralist, and the novel-reader in search of popular entertainment.

How can this be? What qualities attract this interest, so exceptional in both intensity and range?

There are two aspects of a writer's work with which readers need to be familiar before they can fully grasp its significance: the essential nature of the work and the place it occupies in literature. In these can be found the answers to the questions whether the work is worth reading and why: for its own merit or for its share in the merit of others.

For the Brontë sisters, the study of both these aspects must begin in an account of their lives, which reveal in a very special way the source of the unique qualities of their work and of their personal fascination, as well as their place in time and in relation to other writers.

II. LIVES OF THE BRONTËS

The Brontës' father, Patrick Branty or Brunty, was born in northern Ireland in 1777, the eldest of the ten children of a peasant farmer living in a small whitewashed cabin in a soft green dale. Patrick earned his living as blacksmith and linen weaver while scarcely more than a child, and by the time he was sixteen acted as schoolmaster in a tiny village school nearby. He then became tutor to the sons of a neighbouring clergyman with Methodist leanings, who coached the clever lad, helped him to save money and guided him to the University of Cambridge, which he entered as a sizar (that is, a student receiving assistance on the ground of poverty in return for certain services) in 1802. He took his degree in 1806, was ordained a clergyman of the Church of England, and held two curacies. Presently a noted Methodist at his second curacy, a patron of his friend William Morgan, recommended Mr Brontë (as Patrick began to sign himself after the great Nelson became Duke of Brontë) to the vicar of Dewsbury, in the West Riding of Yorkshire, and in 1809 Mr Brontë came to Yorkshire and never afterwards left it as a place of residence. In 1811 William Morgan followed him to Yorkshire, and introduced him to the family of his fiancée, whose father was head of a Wesleyan Methodist school outside Bradford. Here was staying Miss Maria Branwell, a recently orphaned young cousin from Cornwall. Mr Brontë and Miss Branwell fell in love and after a decorous courtship enlivened by charming letters from Maria, married in 1812, Mr Brontë being at that time minister at Hartshead. Six children were born of the marriage in rapid succession: in Hartshead, Maria (1813) and Elizabeth (1815); in Thornton, a remote and hilly village north-west of Bradford, Charlotte (1816), Patrick Branwell (1817), Emily Jane (1818) and Anne (1820). In 1820 Mr Brontë became incumbent of Haworth, a still more remote village, farther to the north-west and therefore set amongst the higher and wilder hills of the Pennine Range; in 1821 Mrs Brontë died, and her sister Elizabeth Branwell from Cornwall stayed in Haworth to look after the motherless children.

These facts already constitute a series of important clues to the understanding of the Brontës. It will be observed that their parents, born in Ireland and Cornwall respectively, were both of Celtic stock, and both Patrick and Maria had a good measure of the picturesque eloquence, the flowing ease of speech, which is one of the Celtic characteristics. Both had been touched by the revival of religious fervour and enthusiasm begun in England by John Wesley and his Methodist followers in the previous century. Maria Branwell's family were prominent Methodists in a county where Methodism had strong hold, while Mr Brontë, though never a professed Methodist, and not given to emotional piety, was in his youth an earnest Evangelical clergyman frequenting Methodist society, whose phrases in his early writings often echo contemporary Methodist speech. His children, except the pious gentle Anne, show hostility to Methodism, perhaps because their somewhat rigid and narrow aunt professed it, perhaps because by their day the separation between Methodism and the Established Anglican Church had become more definite, and Methodist chapel and school formed a kind of opposition to their father's Anglican ministry in Haworth. But a strong religious feeling, coupled with the belief in self-improvement by reading and study which Wesley inculcated, characterized the Brontë household climate during their early formative years.

Mr Brontë in his youth had literary ambitions, and published in Bradford and neighbouring towns two prose tales, two volumes of poems, three pamphlets and a couple of sermons. His wife, too, before her marriage wrote with a view to publication in some periodical an essay entitled 'On the Advantages of Poverty in Religious Concerns'. Frankly, none of these productions has any intrinsic merit, but they are important as bringing the idea of writing for the Press into the Brontë household; the selection of type, the sight of one's name on the title page, the correction of proofs were familiar notions to the little Brontës, so that they 'very early cherished the dream of one day becoming authors'.

It was his belief in education which caused Mr. Brontë after his wife's death to send his eldest four children to a boarding-school for the daughters of clergymen, founded by a clergyman in the neighbouring county of Westmorland. The rigorous discipline and harsh discomfort at Cowan Bridge developed the seeds of consumption latent in Maria and Elizabeth, and after a year there, in 1825, the poor children both died. But the notion that the Brontë sisters were ignorant and unlettered and that their genius flowered out of nothing, is quite erroneous; Mr Brontë took in newspapers and magazines and encouraged his children in self-culture; they belonged to a circulating library in the nearest town and read omnivorously. A list of books which Charlotte at the age of eighteen recommends for a friend's perusal contains works by Scott, Byron, Wordsworth, and Southey, as well as Shakespeare, Milton, Goldsmith, Pope, and many others. It is significant that she says of Pope: 'I don't admire him'. Charlotte and Branwell in their early twenties wrote to Wordsworth and Southey begging opinions on their writings, while Branwell similarly addressed himself to the son of Coleridge. Clearly the young

Brontës were very familiar with the works of the 'Romantic Movement' writers who had inaugurated the new century, and found themselves responsive to the ardour and naturalism of these romantics, as opposed to the formalism of the classic school represented by Pope. (They scarcely ever, for example, use the classic heroic couplet in their verse.)

An important point about the Brontë parents is that they had no relatives near at hand, with the exception of Mrs Brontë's cousin, in whose home the children stayed in early life. Soon, however, she died, and the Brontës were left isolated; they never formed part of a family group and had no kin nearby with whom to visit.

This loneliness was accentuated, and an original turn given to the bent of the children's minds, when the family moved to Haworth Parsonage.

To grasp what Haworth meant in the Brontë children's lives, it is necessary to know something of the geography, industrial history and people of the West Riding of Yorkshire.

This district is filled with the surging heather-topped hills of the Pennine Chain, the rocky spine of England, which runs due north and south for one hundred and fifty miles from the Scottish border. Poor farming land, but amply provided with sheep and streams, the West Riding had for some five hundred years been the seat of a woollen cloth manufacture, which was in process of mechanizing itself precisely at the time when Patrick Brontë entered Yorkshire. Some of the more skilled cloth workers resisted the introduction of machinery which threatened, as they thought, to deprive them of employment; forming themselves into bands known as Luddites, they attacked the inventors and owners of the new machines and the mills where they were housed. This resistance was acute in and about Hartshead in 1812, when Patrick Brontë was curate of that parish. But the workers could not stem the tide of progress; textile mechanization spread rapidly to all branches of the industry and led the way to the general Industrial Revolution.

Haworth was therefore in a state of transition during the early part of the Brontës' lives. Surrounded by wild tracts of moorland and innumerable steep interlocking hills, the people of Haworth communicated with the outer world only by walking, by a carrier's cart or by a hired gig; but the railway came to Keighley and Hebden Bridge, four miles and ten miles away respectively, in the 1840s. Up in the folds of the hills, at the end of rough stony pack-horse tracks, still lived farmers and hand-loom weavers of fiercely independent character, who had never had any master save themselves; but down in the valley three large mechanized mills were at work, busily creating on the one hand a class of wage-earning operatives, on the other the new industrial middle class, rising to wealth on the wings of steam and aspiring to gentility with the characteristic ostentation of the *nouveau riche*.

Because of its isolation, Haworth remained intensely Yorkshire. The Brontës were bilingual, writing Irish brogue or Yorkshire dialect with equal ease; they were also, so to say, bilingual in mind. The Yorkshire character (descended partially from Scandinavian elements) forms a great contrast to the Irish; it is vigorous, practical, prosaic, stubborn, broadly humorous and sparing of speech where the Irish is melancholy, passionate, proud, restless, eloquent, and witty. This striking contrast between the Brontës' heredity and their environment played, as we shall see, a highly important part in forming the nature of their work.

A somewhat stern and dominant father, a strict aunt and a lack of suitable young society threw the Brontës entirely on their own devices for solace and amusement. The moors which surged around them formed the children's great resource. The purple heather, the black rock, the pale tough grass, the bold sweeping contours, offered an aesthetic pleasure which moulded their taste to a fine austerity; the untouched moorland wildness, the strong winds ever blowing there powerfully and freely, provided a moral inspiration. On the moors one could escape from all conventional restraint, and battle freely with earth and sky. These moors exalted the spirit of the Brontës, nourished in their souls the love of liberty. Especially was this the case with the reserved Emily, who, 'stronger than a man, simpler than a child' in Charlotte's estimation, was 'a native and nursling of the moors . . . they were what she lived in and by as much as the wild birds, their tenants, or as the heather, their produce. . . . Liberty was the breath of Emily's nostrils.' It would seem that Emily's poetry derived its austerely magnificent cadence, and her philosophy its 'space-sweeping' vision, from this wild and sombre moorland which she so deeply loved.

The children's other great pleasure lay in the creations of their own minds. A box of wooden soldiers given to Branwell provided the starting-point for a whole day-dream world, where these soldiers, animated into heroes, underwent thrilling adventures and founded a series of kingdoms, known as the Glass Town Confederacy, on the coast of Africa. The four little Brontës, the four Chief Genii of this 'world below', not only invented these brilliantly contrived adventures but recorded them in prose and verse—stories, biographies, magazines, poems lyric and epic—in tiny handwriting on tiny hand-made booklets, whose pages were sometimes only five by three centimetres in size. Presently the children divided into pairs: Charlotte and Branwell created another Glass Town kingdom, Angria, to be conquered and ruled by their favourite Duke of Zamorna and his wicked father-in-law Northangerland, while Emily and Anne withdrew to an imaginary island in the North Pacific named Gondal, the climate of which singularly resembled that of Haworth. The adventures of the stern Queen of Gondal, wild and wicked, were recognized as such without apology; in Angria, however, the many illicit love affairs of the Byronic Zamorna were condoned and slyly enjoyed because forbidden by convention, and the continual treacheries of Northangerland expressed the deep rebellion of Branwell's heart. Angria was, in fact, a 'wish-fulfilment' world, a day-dream in the Freudian sense, its events tainted with neurotic unreality. Charlotte continued these written inventions at least till she was twenty-three, and recurred to them in thought when she was twenty-six, though always with a sense of guilt. Emily, as far as can be judged, continued them freely and serenely all her life. Of the Gondal writings of Emily and Anne only poems are extant, though prose works on Gondal subjects are named by both sisters. Of Charlotte's and Branwell's Angrian booklets there survive enough to contain a wordage equal in length to the whole of the Brontës' published works. Now scattered about England and America and only recently subjected to scholarly collation and research, they form a unique record, invaluable to the student of the Brontës, to the critic interested in the literary creative process and to the psychiatrist, and fascinating in itself, for the Angrian world is created with extraordinary completeness and the characters are warm with life. The clues they provide to the psychological make-up of their ambitious, ardent, over-repressed creators are of the first importance.

Never sent to school, but taught by his father in the intervals of parish work, the unhappy Branwell probably owes much of his ill fate to excessive opportunity for Angrian composition. Real life is bleak to the day-dreamer emerging from his world of fantasy, and after presiding at Cabinet meetings and winning battles in Angria, Branwell found Haworth an intolerable boredom, which it took drink and low company to assuage. As a boy he showed great promise both as writer and painter, but his ambitions remained unfulfilled, partly no doubt from lack of proper tuition (in painting) and guidance, but mainly from defects of character, lack of perseverance and indulgence in dissipation. After a costly experiment with a studio in Bradford he became a tutor, a clerk on the railway, then a tutor again in the same household as Anne.

Meanwhile his sisters were more fortunate. All of them

attended for varying periods a reputable little boarding-school kept by a Miss Wooler in the district already noted as being the scene of Luddite riots. Here Charlotte made that lifelong friendship with a West Riding girl, Ellen Nussey, to which we owe the hundreds of Charlotte's letters which tell the story of the Brontës. Here, too, Charlotte discovered her own ability to learn and teach, and the opportunities of earning a living by teaching offered by this industrial world where the new middle class eagerly sought genteel education for their children. Thenceforward the Brontë sisters for a space of ten years (1835–45) made valiant efforts to gain their livelihood by teaching. Charlotte was twice, and Anne twice, governess in private families, where their experiences furnished material for poignant scenes in their future novels. Even Emily, who had been obliged to leave Miss Wooler's because absence from the moors broke her health, taught in a girls' school for six agonizing months before giving up the struggle. Since they found themselves wretched when away from home and separated from each other, they determined to establish a school of their own, and it was to secure additional qualifications for this that Charlotte and Emily went in 1842 to Brussels, to the *pensionnat de demoiselles* of M. and Mme Heger, to study French and German.

Just preceding this adventure, the youngest sister, the quiet, gentle, pious Anne, underwent one of the formative experiences of her life. Mr Brontë applied successfully for a grant from the Pastoral Aid Society, and the second of his curates, Mr William Weightman, came to Haworth in 1840. This lively, kindly, clever young fellow flirted light-heartedly with all the girls in the neighbourhood, including the Brontës. Anne loved him, and Charlotte gives an amusing account of his 'looking out of the corners of his eyes' at her in church, which shows that he certainly paid her attention. He died of consumption in 1842 while the elder girls were absent in Brussels; some of Anne's poems reveal her quiet mourning for his loss.

In Brussels Charlotte and Emily found the difference in religion and customs from those of Evangelical Yorkshire difficult, and though they made excellent progress in French language and composition they did not in any real sense assimilate the continental culture or way of thought. On Emily the year's sojourn left little trace, unless we accept the hypothesis that the German tales she read there gave elements to *Wuthering Heights*; but on Charlotte the effect was profound. To her, M. Constantin Heger, a fine teacher and a dominating, fiery, irascible, benevolent little man, whose word in the *pensionnat* was law, appeared as a Zamorna translated into terms of real life, a Zamorna respectabilized, modernized, made flesh and blood. That the devotion she felt for him was a sort of delayed schoolgirl's *schwärmerei* is undoubtedly true, but she was a young woman of twenty-six, not a schoolgirl, and the letters she wrote to him later reveal a passion which is all the more poignant for being not quite conscious of its own nature. The girls were summoned home in the autumn by the death of their aunt, but Charlotte 'prompted by what then seemed an irresistible impulse' returned in 1843 and spent a wretched year as pupil-teacher in the *pensionnat*—wretched because as a teacher she now had little contact with her adored master. A terrible holiday spent alone in the *pensionnat* except for a detested colleague, the increasing coolness of the perceptive Mme Heger, and the failing sight of Mr Brontë, determined Charlotte to return to Haworth in early 1844.

Before the day-dream writings were studied it used to be said that M. Heger awakened Charlotte's genius. This is not so; her literary genius was awake and fertile from 1829. But M. Heger's part in her work is still immensely important, for he drew her and her creations out of the shadowy and lurid realms of dreamland into the daylight of the real world.

This point seems to gain emphasis, and M. Heger's integrity its due appreciation, when we see the converse fate which befell Branwell. He, too, fell in love, or so he said— like his Northangerland, that Byronic hero 'bright with beauty, dark with crime'—within forbidden limits, namely with his employer's wife, Mrs Robinson; but unlike Charlotte he thought he received encouragement. Whatever the truth of this umbrageous episode—Branwell was a compulsive boaster and liar—Mr Robinson certainly dismissed him with contumely, though without any clear accusation, in the summer of 1845. The poor foolish lad now decayed rapidly in morals and health; he took to opium and brandy, ran so gravely into debt that the Sheriff's officer pursued him to the Parsonage; raved luridly through the nights and dozed in stupor by day.

His sisters' school project (which in any case had shown no signs of prospering) had perforce to be abandoned, and they now all remained at home together, to sustain their father and each other through this trial. It was during this period, and thus as a direct consequence of poor Branwell's tragedy, that Charlotte 'accidentally lighted on' a manuscript volume of verse in Emily's handwriting. Of recent years the sisters had not shown each other what they wrote, and accordingly Charlotte was intensely struck by the power, the originality, and the wild melancholy music of Emily's poems, and thought at once of publication. The reserved Emily was furious at her sister's intrusion into her private life, but the gentle Anne produced some of her own verses, and eventually Charlotte secured Emily's consent to the publication of a volume of poems by all three sisters. 'Averse to personal publicity', says Charlotte, 'we veiled our own names under those of Currer, Ellis, and Acton Bell.' She explains that these 'ambiguous' names, which might indeed belong to persons of either sex, were chosen because the girls had a 'scruple at assuming Christian names positively masculine', yet wished to avoid the condescension or derision with which reviewers then often treated women writers. Part of their little legacies from Aunt Branwell paid for the volume, which was published in the summer of 1846. Except for one review, which spoke of Ellis Bell's 'evident power of wing', it was little noticed, and only two copies were sold. Before transferring the remainder of the edition 'to the trunk-makers' for lining, Charlotte later sent copies to Words-worth, Lockhart, De Quincey, and Tennyson.

But the sight of one's words in print, whether they are well received or no, is stimulating to the true author, and the three sisters each set to work to write—or to finish writing—a work of fiction. Charlotte's first novel was *The Professor*, Anne's *Agnes Grey*, Emily's her solitary but superb masterpiece, *Wuthering Heights*. For some eighteen months, Charlotte tells us, these novels, which were shorter than the three-volume length then requisite, were 'per-severingly obtruded upon various publishers', receiving in each case 'an ignominious and abrupt refusal'. At length the novels of the younger two sisters were accepted 'on terms somewhat impoverishing to the authors', but *The Professor* remained without a home. Meanwhile Mr Brontë's cataract grew ready for the operation; Charlotte accom-panied him to Manchester for this purpose, and while there began to write *Jane Eyre*. Venturing forth her first born yet once again she found it refused by Messrs Smith, Elder in terms so courteous and discriminating that she took fresh courage, and when *Jane Eyre* was finished sent it to them. They accepted it with enthusiasm and published it within six weeks; appearing in October 1847, it achieved a high and lasting success. Meanwhile *Wuthering Heights* and *Agnes Grey* yet lingered in the press. Stimulated by the success of *Jane Eyre*, their publisher brought them out in December, but Anne's fiction was overlooked, while Mr Ellis Bell was characterized as 'dogged, brutal, and morose'. Anne, however, with quiet courage began another novel, *The Tenant of Wildfell Hall*, and Charlotte planned *Shirley*, while Messrs Smith, Elder bought up the unbound sheets of the *Poems* and prepared to nurse carefully and enthu-siastically the reputation of the three Bells. It seemed as if the sun would at last come out over Haworth Parsonage.

But it was not to be. Branwell, whose sisters kept the secret of their publications from him so as not to rub salt

in the wounds of his failure, deteriorated rapidly in health
and died in September 1848. The passing of this once so
promising, ambitious, and beloved brother was an anguish
to all three sisters, who were too noble-minded to allow
themselves to dwell on the release it brought. Emily caught
cold at his funeral; her illness was no doubt increased by
psychological causes; she tried to dominate the consumption
which supervened by her stern will, failed, and died in
December of the same year. Scarcely was she buried when
Anne, her close companion always, showed signs of the
same mortal disease. She died at the Yorkshire seaside
resort of Scarborough in May 1849.

Poor Charlotte's life was thenceforward lived, so to speak,
in two distinct and scarcely communicating compartments.
At home she dwelt in silence, solitude, an ever-deepening
loneliness. She finished *Shirley*, which was received with
acclaim, with fair rapidity, but needed three years of des-
perate struggle to write *Villette*. In London, on the other
hand, which she visited once yearly, she was lionized under
the skilful management of the agreeable young George
Smith. A *tendresse* arose between Smith and herself, which
however, dissimilarity in family connexions, social position
and age prevented from any consummation. A subordinate
member of the firm, James Taylor, loved Charlotte and
came to Haworth Parsonage intending probably to offer
for her hand; but when she saw him in home surroundings
her 'veins ran ice' and she was unable to encourage him to
make the proposal. He went out to India to represent the
Smith, Elder firm, presently married there and died there
twenty years later.

Luckily for posterity, one of the literary friendships
Charlotte made during this period was with the novelist Mrs
Gaskell, who afterwards wrote the admirable *Life of Charlotte
Brontë*, one of the finest biographies in the English language.

Meanwhile another suitor arose for Charlotte near at
hand: her father's curate, the Northern Irishman Arthur
Bell Nicholls. Earnest, conscientious, kind but narrow, not

gifted with 'fine talents, congenial tastes and thoughts',
Nicholls won Charlotte's consent at last by loving her, not
as a writer—he detested the Brontës' literary fame—but as
a woman. Mr Brontë ill-advisedly objected to his suit on
snobbish grounds, which threw the generous Charlotte's
sympathies on his side. Nicholls left Haworth for a time
but corresponded with Charlotte, and eventually—his
successor as curate proving very unsatisfactory to Mr
Brontë—won her father's consent and her own. They
were married in June 1854, and after honeymooning in
Ireland took up residence with Mr Brontë at the Parsonage.
Charlotte's letters at this time, though full of praise for her
kind and considerate husband, have moments of great
poignancy: 'The colour of my thoughts is a good deal
changed . . . it is a solemn and strange and perilous thing
for a woman to become a wife'.

In the following winter she became pregnant, and died in
March 1855, from *hyperemesis gravidarum* (i.e. excessive
sickness in pregnancy), heightened by the Brontës' old
enemy phthisis. The appearance of Mrs Gaskell's biography
in 1857, the posthumous publication of *The Professor* in the
same year and the death of old Mr Brontë in 1861 after
six years' conscientious if somewhat dominating attendance
by Mr Nicholls, complete the Brontë chronicle.

From the materials provided, and with minds created and
formed, by these events, we have seen that the Brontë
sisters wrote seven novels and some four hundred poems.

III. CHARLOTTE BRONTË

Charlotte's verse is not important in itself, but it illumin-
ates her strange personal history and the debt we owe to
M. Heger for drawing her out of her shadow world. Her
poems fall into two categories. The larger part are Angrian,

i.e. poems written as if by Angrian characters in Angrian situations. These, though fascinating to the psychologist, strike me as a sheer waste of talent; since events in Angria, with its fantasies of resuscitation and wish-fulfilment, are essentially false to the truth of life. The attempt to evoke emotion on their behalf is consciously false and produces no response in the reader. So true is this that when in the 1846 Bell *Poems* Charlotte substitutes real names and places for Angrian ones for the purpose of publication, the falsity of the feeling still strikes uneasily through. Yet in these Angrian compositions—for example, 'Zamorna's Exile', a long narrative poem in the Byronic stanza (a b a b a b c c) and the last half of 'Retrospection'—Charlotte's technical facility is at its best. In the other category, poems of real life, when writing of personal experiences—in 'Life', 'The Teacher's Monologue', 'Parting', the tragic Hegerian 'He Saw my Heart's Woe', and so on—Charlotte sometimes achieves a grave poignancy of feeling and dignity of phrase. Especially is this the case in the first part of 'Retrospection', beginning 'We Wove a Web in Childhood', where she describes in symbolic terms the creation of their dream-worlds by the Brontë children. But in general, her verse is novelist's verse, tending to narrative and incident rather than to lyrical intensity and when she found her real *métier* in fiction she dropped the writing of poetry.

For Charlotte is essentially a novelist. Her childhood Angrian stories already show an admirable skill in construction, characterization, and narration, an enviable fertility in incident. In *The Professor* for the first time she intended to transfer these abilities to a fiction of real life, and it is interesting to mark her efforts to effect the transition from day-dream to daylight. She tells us in a preface prepared for a suggested issue of the book during her lifetime:

... in many a crude effort ... I had got over any such taste as I might once have had for ornamented and redundant composition, and come to prefer what was plain and homely. At the same time I had adopted a

set of principles on the subject of incident etc. . . . . I said to myself that
my hero should work his way through life as I had seen real living men
work theirs—that he should never get a shilling he had not earned—
that no sudden turns should lift him in a moment to wealth and high
station . . . he should not even marry a beautiful girl or a lady of rank.
As Adam's son he should share Adam's doom, and drain throughout
life a mixed and moderate cup of enjoyment.

Preface to The Professor

This relentless truthfulness to ordinary reality is to prove
one of the main characteristics of Charlotte's best fiction.
But *The Professor*, having opened with an overdrawn hatred-
between-two-brothers sequence taken straight out of
Angria, then swings somewhat too violently away from the
picturesque to the prosaic, so that its realism seems sometimes
so full of gall as to reject digestion. Yet the book has striking
originality, power, and promise.

The orphaned William Crimsworth, rejected by his
aristocratic uncles and his sordid mill-owner brother, goes
to Brussels and secures a post as teacher in a boys' school.
Presently he is invited to give lessons in the girls' school
next door, kept by the smooth but hypocritical Mlle
Zoraïde. In this establishment he meets a young pupil
teacher, Frances Henri by name, Swiss Protestant by descent.
Crimsworth and Frances come to love each other. Mlle
Zoraïde, though betrothed to Crimsworth's employer,
succeeds in separating the lovers for a while, but presently
they meet again, marry, start a school of their own, achieve
a competence and retire to England with their child Victor,
who in accordance with the saturnine mood of the whole
novel 'is as little of a pretty child as I am of a handsome man,
or his mother of a fine woman'.

The master-pupil relationship Charlotte experienced in
Brussels, used in *The Professor* for the first time, is here told
with nationalities reversed. Charlotte's own opinion of this
novel, written later, at the time of a proposed publication,
could hardly be improved on as a critical estimate:

I found the beginning very feeble, the whole narrative deficient in incident and in general attractiveness. Yet . . . all that relates to Brussels, the Belgian school etc. is as good as I can write . . . it contains more pith, more substance, more reality, in my judgment than much of *Jane Eyre*. It gives, I think, a new view of a grade, an occupation, and a class of characters—all very commonplace, very insignificant in themselves.

Letter, 14 December 1847

Here we strike upon the keynote of Charlotte's work. It is the respectable powerless, the poor genteel, the 'patient and persecuted stranger' of noble integrity, whom she always chooses as her protagonist. Spiritual integrity holding its own against a purse-proud world, a matter pressed upon the attention of the poor parson's daughter by the Industrial Revolution, is the invariable theme of her work.

In *Jane Eyre* (1847), the most popular, as reading and publishing statistics show, of all the Brontë novels, Charlotte achieved a perfect fusion of realism and romance.

We first meet ugly, unhappy little Jane as the despised orphan in the house of her uncle's widow. Hounded into rebellion, she is packed off to a 'charity' boarding-school, her career there queered in advance by her aunt's branding her as a liar. A gentle schoolfellow, Helen Burns, befriends her but soon dies, her latent consumption developed by the harsh school discipline administered with especial rigour by one of the mistresses. Jane sets herself to learn, qualifies herself as a teacher, advertises for a post and finds herself governessing the little illegitimate French daughter of Edward Fairfax Rochester in his country mansion, Thornfield. The master-pupil love relationship develops between the *farouche*, dominant Rochester and Jane; her resolute free spirit, her soul of fire, bring from him a proposal of marriage, but at the very altar the wedding ceremony is interrupted, and we discover the secret which has been skilfully hinted, that Thornfield harbours a mad woman who is

Rochester's wife. Implored to join her life to Rochester's as his mistress, Jane resolutely refuses and leaves the house, penniless. She wanders far away, is rescued by the Rivers family and urged to marry the frigid St John Rivers in order to undertake missionary work at his side; almost she consents, but as she ponders, Rochester's voice crying her name resounds in her ears. She returns to Thornfield; it is in ruins, destroyed by a fire started by the mad wife who perished in the flames. In a secluded country house near by she finds Rochester, blind and alone; they marry and find happiness together.

The reason for *Jane Eyre's* popularity with the ordinary reader is not far to seek. It embodies two age-old human stories, two basic folk-themes: the Cinderella story (poor oppressed girl marries powerful prince) and the success story (new arrival suffers, perseveres, and triumphs). These stories persist in human history because they express permanent human aspirations; for while most men wish to be powerfully protective to their women, most women wish to marry powerfully protective men, and everyone wishes to succeed in new ventures. But why did this novel, why does it still, receive the approbation of critics?

To begin with, the story is told with terrific intensity. The agonies of Jane, the death of Helen, the exquisite love scenes, are presented so powerfully and poignantly, in such simple but telling language, that they cannot be read without emotion. Then, *Jane Eyre* is not a mere 'escape' romance; it has a determined truth and honesty of its own. Even when the action is most exciting, its details (as in real life) are firmly prosaic, and Jane does not enjoy a complete, unreal triumph; she does not end as a rich beauty, all difficulties past, but as the plain (though happy) wife of an exacting, half-blind, disgraced husband with a highly inconvenient daughter. In a word, as a human being she shares the true human fate, and 'drains but a mixed and moderate cup of enjoyment'.

Last—and most important—*Jane Eyre* is the first English

novel, and perhaps even yet the most powerful and popular novel, which presents the new, the modern, and surely the permanently true view of woman's position in the social fabric. In a series of superb scenes with the powerful and wealthy Rochester, the poor but independent Jane presses passionately upon him her conviction that she is his equal, that she has as much mind and soul as he and more heart, that she will follow the dictates of her conscience without fear, that she can earn her own living and 'need not sell her soul to buy bliss', that she has 'an inward treasure' which will sustain her in all circumstances. Jane is not afraid to tell Rochester frankly that she loves him, that wherever he is, there is her home, but that she despises him for thinking of marrying a rich and beautiful but spiritually inferior girl. In 1847 such an attitude was an astonishment and a portent; even today it is not as generally accepted as could be wished. Jane is all woman and all women, but bends upon the woman's eternal problem of love versus society her mind as well as her heart.

Shirley (1849) strikes quite a different note. A story of the Yorkshire Luddite riots of 1812, it is one of the first two great regional novels, and one of the first two great industrial novels, in English literature, sharing the honour of originality in these subjects with Mrs Gaskell's *Mary Barton*, a Lancashire industrial tale which was composed during many of the same months as *Shirley* and published in the previous year.

Every facet of Yorkshire's industrial problem in 1812 is admirably expressed in Charlotte's story. Robert Moore, the cloth manufacturer of Hollow's Mill, the half-Belgian, half-Yorkshire descendant of an old mercantile house, is faced with bankruptcy, because the war between England and Napoleon has cut off his continental markets. The new textile machinery, which by eliminating some labour and speeding up the processes will cheapen his product, may save him from ruin; accordingly he is determined to install it whatever the sufferings of his discharged operatives. These men in despair turn Luddite, break his machines as they cross the moor, attack his mill, shoot and wound him from behind a hedge. He is saved from ruin only by a loan from the young heiress Shirley Keeldar, who however rejects his mercenary proposal of marriage with scorn and marries his tutor brother Louis, thus leaving the repentant Moore free to marry his true love, Caroline Helstone, the vicar's niece. Subsidiary complications, all however skilfully linked to the main theme, introduce Caroline's long-lost mother, a Radical mill-owner's family, various vicars, old maids, workmen, Methodists, baronets, indeed members of all classes of society in the neighbourhood, together with three curates, famous in fiction because drawn with such devasta- ting though humorous realism.

Shirley is an immensely vigorous and large-scale creation, pulsating with life and offering a wonderful range of characters, all actively at work in house, road, church, mill, in the full daylight of realistic presentation. As a picture of Yorkshire life in the 1840s (for no meticulous historical detail of 1812 overweights the story) it is supreme, and the portraits of Hiram Yorke and Joe Scott are as true of West Riding millowners and foremen today as they were a century ago. The fiercely independent Hiram, who can speak both good English and broad Yorkshire when he chooses, becomes ever broader in his speech the higher the rank of the person he addresses and the more he dislikes him; while Joe Scott's remarks on the sharp wits of northern mechanics and the mincing speech of the 'grand folk fro' London' have remained entirely contemporary through a hundred years. But Charlotte hesitated over the title of *Shirley* and this hesitation was symptomatic; the novel lacks unity of theme. There are two master-pupil relationships, Shirley and Louis, Caroline and Robert, and the interest veers between the two girls. Shirley (said to be a portrait of Emily Brontë as she might have been if rich and free) is frank and proud, lithe, quick, energetic in mind and body, generous, ardent, and bold; a 'sister of the spotted, bright, quick, fiery leopard', she would have burst any other novel of the period asunder by sheer force of vitality. The influence of Shirley on Yorkshire life and Yorkshire women is still strong, and many daughters of intelligent and independent-minded women are named after her to-day. Caroline (partly drawn from Ellen Nussey) is entirely different: gentle, sweet, ladylike, modest, a girl of her century, she slowly and agonizingly breaks her heart for Robert, longing for work to help her subdue her grief, but unable to break out of the narrow circle of convention which encloses her. Except for this pathetic study of a breaking heart, Shirley is more 'external' than any other of Charlotte's novels, and there is a certain amount of conversational 'padding' to bring the tale up to three-volume length. Yorkshire landscape, described here and there as vignettes in The Professor and Jane Eyre, in Shirley naturally enough receives fuller treatment, but it is less the wild moorland of Haworth than the wooded undulations round Hartshead.

Villette (1853) is regarded by many good critics, though not by the general public, as Charlotte's finest novel. Certainly if The Professor be forgotten its originality is great, while its study of a woman's loneliness is supreme.

The disappointments of Villette are doubtless due to the rigid convention of the day respecting the proper length for a novel, which obliged Charlotte to make a four-strand plot out of a single-strand story. The core of the book is Charlotte's Brussels experience—Villette being the name she gives to the city of Brussels—in the Heger pensionnat, here presented boldly in close resemblance to its actual fact. Lucy Snowe arrives by night, practically penniless, in Villette, is taken on by Mme Beck as her children's nurse on the judgement of her kinsman and English professor, M. Paul Emanuel, and presently becomes English teacher in her school. The pupil-teacher love-relationship develops between Lucy and M. Paul. During the holidays Lucy is left alone at the *pensionnat* except for an idiot girl; in agonizing loneliness she roams the streets, enters a Catholic Church, makes—fierce little Protestant that she is—a confession to a priest. Later M. Paul realizes his love for her and wishes to marry her; but the jealous Mme Beck stimulates the religious difficulty to keep them apart, and when that proves inadequate packs M. Paul off to Guadaloupe to attend to family affairs. Before he goes, however, M. Paul establishes Lucy in a neat tiny school of her own, and promises to return in three years. A storm wrecks his ship on return and poor Lucy's hopes.

Now all this part of *Villette* belongs to a very high creative level; it is strongly original and effective. The character-drawing is superb. M. Paul—that 'magnificent-minded, grand-hearted, dear, faulty little man', irritable, fussy, intelligent, and noble, with his facial resemblance to 'a black and sallow tiger' and his temper to match—is a wonderful creation, intensely original, intensely living. Mme Beck, a 'compact little pony' with an ever-neat, fresh appearance, an admirable manager, bland and decorous, who wears list slippers so that she may the more easily spy, is equally new in fiction and equally striking. Lucy herself is a magnificent study, though exasperating as a person— which accounts for her comparative unpopularity among Charlotte's heroines. Independent, alone, poor, and proud, ice without, fire within, she is in fact a Puritan, a masochist who often denies herself what her ardent soul craves, on principle, believes that it is part of God's plan that 'some must deeply suffer while they live', and thrills to know herself one of their number. 'Dark through the wilderness of this world stretches the way for most of us; equal and steady be our tread; be our cross our banner.' The intensity of Lucy's feeling, whether of abandonment, loneliness, despair or love, in the rain outside Mme Beck's door or on her knees at the confessional, and the wild poetry of their expression, sweep the reader away on the tide of complete conviction. If *Shirley* lies at the Yorkshire end of

Charlotte's gamut, *Villette* lies at the other, the Celtic, extreme.

Unfortunately around this core, their interrelations rather too neatly and skilfully arranged, circle three other groups: the Brettons, mother and son; the Home de Bassompierres, father and daughter; Ginevra Fanshawe and her mysterious suitor. Though Lucy at one time loves Dr John Bretton, her godmother's son, and has to watch him first entangled with the lazy, pretty Ginevra and then seriously in love with the strange elfin Pauline Home, the reader never quite believes in her feeling for him and does not care what happens to it; all these subsidiary characters in these minor plots are invented rather than created, or rather, drawn too directly from Charlotte's recent experiences with her publisher George Smith, and insufficiently re-created. But Lucy, Professor Paul, Madame Beck, and the terrible emotional intensity of the woman alone, maintaining her integrity against the world, are unique and splendid achievements.

IV. WORKS OF EMILY BRONTË

The poems of Emily Brontë, and her novel *Wuthering Heights*, little regarded at the time of their publication, have now come to be considered amongst the noblest productions of English literature.

Many of her poems are Gondal poems, but since Gondal was a wish-fulfilment fiction certainly, but not a neurotic fantasy like Angria, this does not vitiate their content or appeal; whether Emily writes in the person of a Gondal queen or a harassed Yorkshire teacher is no matter: the emotions presented are always deeply true to life. Moreover, we have to be grateful to Gondal for some of her finest poems, such as 'To Imagination', 'Plead for Me', 'The

Visionary', and others, where she magnificently defends her imagination, the creator of Gondal ('My slave, my comrade and my king') against the arguments of reason and the less noble pursuits of the real world:\

> He comes with western winds, with evening's wandering airs,
> With that clear dusk of heaven that brings the thickest stars,
> Winds take a pensive tone, and stars a tender fire,
> And visions rise, and change, that kill me with desire.

There are two elements in Emily's poetry whose fusion provides its special personal quality: the local and the universal. Her descriptions of her beloved moorlands have not merely a vividly pictorial but a profound emotional effect. Such lines as:

> Where the grey flocks in ferny glens are feeding,
> Where the wild wind blows on the mountain side.

or:

> . . . in the red fire's cheerful glow
> I think of deep glens, blocked with snow;
> I dream of moor, and misty hill,
> Where evening closes dark and chill . . .

evoke in the hearts of those who love the moors a deep nostalgic emotion.

But though Emily does not scorn to hymn the sheep, the heather and the bluebell of the West Riding countryside, she has also a 'space-sweeping soul'; she deals greatly with great human themes. Courage, compassion and what some critics call mysticism, but I myself prefer to analyse as an awareness of the workings of the cosmos, are the most frequent subjects of her poems. Here are some lines from the famous *Stanzas to* ——, which though written for a Gondal situation probably reveal Emily's feelings towards Branwell, and certainly express that profound but clear-eyed compassion, condemning the deed but not the doer, which characterizes the noblest thinkers of all time:

Do I despise the timid deer,
Because his limbs are fleet with fear?
Or, would I mock the wolf's death-howl,
Because his form is gaunt and foul?
Or, hear with joy the leveret's cry,
Because it cannot bravely die?
No! Then above his memory
Let pity's heart as tender be.

And here are the first verses of Emily's most famous poem, the magnificent lines which express at once her superb courage and her belief in the God of Life:

No coward soul is mine,
    No trembler in the world's storm-troubled sphere:
I see Heaven's glories shine,
    And faith shines equal, arming me from fear.

O God within my breast,
    Almighty, ever-present Deity!
Life—that in me has rest,
    As I—undying Life—have power in Thee!

Vain are the thousand creeds
    That move men's hearts: unutterably vain;
Worthless as withered weeds,
    Or idlest froth amid the boundless main . . .

Emily's language seems to me to have a wonderful heather bloom—that is to say, separately the phrases are dun and simple, but when massed into Emily's mighty pattern they add up to majestic folds of purple. Her words are austere, her metres (though varied) are not new. She scorns elaboration, rejects the glittering adjective, the far-fetched image, the eye-catching flourish; she states her meaning, one feels, as plainly as she can, without any concession to the desire for brilliance. But the strange music of her rhythm and her piercingly exact choice of word give her line that mysterious but potent magic which is the mark of true poetry. As for

the ideas her poems express, far from being now out-
dated they remain still in advance of the thought of our
time.

The same fusion of the local and the universal occurs in
Wuthering Heights (1847), that fierce, wild, strange novel
whose quality is unique in English literature.

The story of *Wuthering Heights* is in essence simple,
concerning two symmetrical families and an intruding
stranger. The Earnshaw family—a bluff prosperous York-
shireman, his wife, his son Hindley, his daughter Catherine—
live in their handsome old family farmhouse, Wuthering
Heights, up in the folds of the moors. (The word 'wuthering' is Yorkshire dialect for 'weathering', 'a significant
provincial adjective', as Emily says ironically, 'descriptive
of the atmospheric tumult to which its station is exposed in
stormy weather'.) The Linton family, richer and more
genteel, landed gentry—Mr Linton, his wife, his son Edgar,
his daughter Isabella—live down in a neighbouring valley
at Thrushcross Grange. One day Mr Earnshaw brings
home to the Heights a sallow, ragged little boy he has found
wandering in the streets of a city which he has visited for
business. To this waif he gives the name of Heathcliff.
The children grow up together; Catherine loves Heathcliff,
while Hindley hates him from jealousy of his father's fond-
ness for the stranger. Mr Earnshaw and his wife die,
Hindley degrades Heathcliff in every way he can; the lad
grows brutal and morose and Catherine turns from him to
the mild Edgar Linton. Heathcliff decamps, to return later
when Catherine is Edgar's wife, rich, and with the manners
of a gentleman concealing his dark fierce heart. Between
Heathcliff and Edgar, Catherine becomes distracted; she
gives birth to Edgar's daughter, Cathy, and dies. Heathcliff
then sets himself to ruin both families in revenge. He turns
Hindley into a drunkard and gambler and wins all his posses-
sions, so that his son Hareton Earnshaw is a pauper in
Heathcliff's house. Heathcliff contrives to marry Edgar
Linton's vain silly sister Isabella, and after her death marries

Linton's daughter Cathy to his own peevish ailing son. But all his revenge is foiled by Cathy and Hareton, who love each other and redeem each other, and by his own affection for Hareton, his old enemy's son.

The clear outlines of this story are often confused in readers' minds by the method Emily employs to tell it, namely in a series of first-person narrations which do not go straight forward in time. She begins the book towards the end of the story, when Heathcliff is apparently triumphant. He owns both Wuthering Heights and Thrushcross Grange, and the descendants of Lintons and Earnshaws are completely in his power. His tenant at Thrushcross Grange, Mr Lockwood, coming to the Heights to call on his landlord, is first perplexed and then made madly curious by the strange behaviour and mysterious relationships of the people he finds living there. The reader, too, is made intensely curious and longs to hear the explanation of it all, which presently Lockwood, before he leaves the neighbourhood in disgust with the climate, hears from the Earnshaws' old nurse, Nellie Dean. Within her narrative come other first-person narratives, of young Cathy and of Isabella. Then later Lockwood comes back again, sees a completely changed situation at the Heights and again hears the explanation from Nellie Dean. This method, complex and one would judge not easy to sustain, renders high dividends in excitement and suspense.

It is worth noticing here that whereas Charlotte's stories, and as we shall see later Anne's, belong essentially to the nineteenth century—which indeed they inaugurate: the century of governesses and machines and trains—so far as Emily's novel belongs to any one time it is that of the eighteenth century—the century of horse transport, rough tracks, remote houses, character unsoftened by urban contacts—which lingered in Emily's day in the Haworth uplands. But in essence Emily's tale is timeless: a tale of elemental, universal passions, love scorned turning into a fury of revenge and hate.

Emily's novel gains its special quality partly from the terrible intensity with which its characters feel these mighty passions. Catherine and Hindley Earnshaw have proud, fierce wilful natures; Heathcliff is almost demoniac in his terrible force of will. All three express their feelings with such awful intensity, such uninhibited force, such untamed violence that one can hardly read of them without a strong shudder of excitement.

Emily Brontë's manner of writing, too, here as in her poems, is austere and unadorned, but mighty; as powerful as the north wind which rages round Wuthering Heights. Such scenes as Catherine's dying farewell to Heathcliff, or that fearful incident when Lockwood dreams he hears her ghost, twenty years later, still wailing at the Wuthering Heights' windows: 'Let me in—let me in!' are almost unbearably moving.

Another most potent element in the novel is its local colouring, which occurs in character, speech, and scene. The setting, the scenery of the book is magnificently Yorkshire. Of the wild and sombre moors which surge round the Heights, Emily gives glorious pictures, in all seasons, in all weathers. She writes of them in winter, when sky and sombre hills are mingled in one bitter whirl of wind and suffocating snow; in spring, when the larks are singing beneath a blue sky and all the becks are full and running with a mellow flow; in summer when the bees are humming dreamily above the purple heather; in the cool of the evening, when beneath a clear spacious sky the pale moths flutter among the blue harebells. The landscape painting in this novel is superb, unrivalled in English fiction.

It is this untamed moorland and its untamed characters who admit no restraint on their fierce passions, which give *Wuthering Heights* its incomparable air of dark, wild, stormy freedom.

But this novel has another, and most noble, element, which as in her poetry fuses with the local to give her work its special quality: Emily's comprehension, spacious as the universe, of the problems of good and evil. Emily shows us, with a full realization of their evil, the weakness of Edgar, the silliness of his sister, the cruelty of Heathcliff, the brutality of Hindley, the egoism of Catherine, as well as the force and pathos of their griefs and their loves. But, as we have seen in her poetry, she does not *blame* faulty mortals for acting in accordance with the nature fate has given them. Neither does she exonerate or excuse them; she simply portrays them—with relentless truth, but also with the compassion induced by limitless understanding. It is as when above the wild and sombre moorland, through the dark storm-driven clouds, appear the serene blue dusk and evening star which belong to the cosmic heavens. The resulting landscape has an incomparable majesty and beauty.

In *Wuthering Heights*, as in her poems, Emily Brontë makes us contemplate, without evasion, some of the most powerful primal human motives, engaged, against a wild, free, stormy background, in ferocious conflict. She does not, I think, make us experience the Aristotelean purge by pity and terror; such emotions are beneath her level of courage. Rather does the lofty grandeur with which she invests this tragic spectacle excite, strengthen and embolden our spirit to be itself more freely and courageously.

V. WORKS OF ANNE BRONTË

Anne Brontë's work not only forms a curious and interesting complement to that of her sisters, but has a certain special flavour of its own.

Looking over her sisters' papers after their death to edit a further selection of their poems, Charlotte says she found 'mournful evidence' of Anne's 'sincere but sorrowing piety'. This still, quiet, sad, almost morbid piety is the special personal characteristic of all Anne's work, which shares its moorland material with Emily, its governessing with Charlotte. Her love for William Weightman, and her frightened abhorrence of Branwell's rackety ways, are again her own peculiar experience, and out of all these she wrote.

Anne is not by any means a major poet. Her ideas lack breadth and boldness; her words lack colour and animation. But both have a certain quiet propriety and precision; grey, mild but inexorable, like soft steady rain, her words express a subdued but real intensity of feeling and steadiness of purpose. Unlike Emily's, her narrative Gondal verses are negligible, but her poems of personal experience deserve attention. Sad little verses commemorate the sunny smile and light heart of Mr Weightman, the poem entitled 'Domestic Peace' reveals how poor Anne suffered from Branwell's destruction of that blessing, and her comments on her governess's lot ('Lines Written at Thorp Green'), her longings for time in which to be herself ('Retirement') and her agonized plea to be called soon to eternity 'if this indeed be all That life can show to me', have a grave still pathos which brings an ache to the reader's heart. Several of her religious poems have found a place in Methodist and Baptist hymnals, especially 'The Three Guides', where Anne analyses and rejects the spirits of Earth and Pride and accepts the Spirit of Faith.

Her first novel, *Agnes Grey* (1847), reveals this same quiet piety, coupled however with a cool eye for domestic hypocrisy. Agnes, the younger daughter of an impoverished clergyman, takes two posts as governess. In the first she is with vulgar *nouveaux riches*, whose rude unruly children spit in her workbag and throw her desk out of the window. In the second, a household of unlettered aristocrats, she has to cope with an insolent coquette and a horsey tomboy. She meets and likes the new curate; the coquette separates them; but eventually cleric and governess meet by chance in Scarborough and decorously become engaged. These little incidents are all narrated in the first person, simply and briefly, in chapters headed: 'The Church', 'The Cottagers', 'The Shower', and so on.

This all sounds very mild, but in fact it has a tang of its own because of Anne's close observation and relentless honesty of narrative. As she tells us herself, she had an 'immutable preference' for 'wholesome truth', for depicting people 'rather as they really are than as they would wish to appear'. Her heroine is endowed with 'ordinary brown hair'; a roué has by no means the romance of a Rochester, but a 'blotchy' face, and is 'disagreeably red about the eyelids'; while a sister's highly approved fiancé is described as merely 'decent' in looks and 'middling' in age. This scorn for false extremes, romantic excesses, is typical of Anne. The scene where, just arrived, Agnes struggles to eat cold tough meat under the eyes of her new employers; the scene where she drops a stone on a nestful of fledglings to prevent her pupils putting them to torture; the awful schoolroom scenes; the curious workings of parental love—all these Anne recounts without, so to speak, ever raising her voice, but with a grave exact simplicity, a precision of detail, which have a quietly devastating effect.

The Tenant of Wildfell Hall (1848) is painted in bolder colours, but with a less certain hand. Anne wrote it to show the evils of drunkenness as she knew them in Branwell, and whenever she is describing the drunkard Arthur Huntingdon on the morning after a debauch, the close accuracy of her observation carries entire conviction. But the debauch itself is from sheer ignorance less well described, and Helen's diary of her wretched marriage to Huntingdon proves less interesting than Gilbert Markham's account of his love for the mysterious new 'tenant', Helen, who has fled from her husband with her little son. A noticeably good feature of this novel is Anne's painting of the moorland landscapes which surround Wildfell Hall. Though they lack the wild poetry which Emily gives to these adored phenomena, Anne's earth and wind and weather are always closely observed from life, and thus have a welcome freshness and truth.

With her perfect spiritual integrity, her quiet scorn for

the worldly, her calm, clear, grey sentences, her still intensity, her truthfulness, her fresh angle on domestic life, Anne is in her own right a minor classic.

VI. CONCLUSION

Emily, a major poet who is also the author of a superb masterpiece of fiction; Charlotte, a novelist of strong and original genius; Anne, a writer of clear if somewhat pallid talent—it is a remarkable trio to come from one family resident in a remote moorland parish in days when female education had hardly begun. Indeed the Brontës' lives form such a poignant and fascinating human document that it is not surprising so much interest has been concentrated upon their personalities. But it is our present business to analyse the nature of their work and estimate its place in literature.

Clearly they are exceptionally powerful story-tellers; original in subject-matter, penetrating in characterization, compelling in narrative. Their fine pictures of Yorkshire life and landscape are their most obvious merit. With Charlotte and Anne a deeper interest is provided by their poignant presentation from within, of the woman humble and insignificant yet nobly independent, finely intelligent, ardently passionate. Charlotte especially seems to me with respect to women to herald, before its dawn, the modern world—one does not meet women such as hers again in English fiction till the turn of the twentieth century. Emily stands alone in her portrayal of timeless and elemental human passions.

But when this has been said, we have not yet explained the Brontës' special claim on our attention, which consists in the unique and beautiful quality, the highly individual flavour, of their work. Although each sister has her own nature, they share this quality in common, though in varying degree.

No other British writer has this quality. It is a strange compound, a unique blend, of poetry with prose, of the wild and free with the domestic, of wisdom with innocence, of irony with intensity, of realism with romance. I suggest that it resulted from the fusion in their spirit of their Celtic heredity with their Yorkshire environment. Yorkshire gave them their robust and relentless realism, their tenacious honesty, their energy, their stubborn belief in equality and freedom; their Celtic parentage provided their ardour, their intensity, their proud melancholy, their flowing speech. The Haworth moorland, their loneliness and suffering intensified the Celtic side of their nature; the prosaic experiences of their Industrial-Revolution Yorkshire lives developed that ironic realism which is so often the woman's defence against stultifying domestic detail. They dealt with the Celtic-Yorkshire psychological situation with varying degrees of success; Charlotte and Branwell were always ill at ease with the diverse elements of their natures, and Charlotte's writing is uneven accordingly. Anne solved the problem by pious resignation, Emily by a spacious vision which easily comprehended both.

Although the Brontës, like all other human phenomena, are necessarily to some extent a product of what went before them, they are not derivative in the usual sense of the word, for as we have seen they added to the ingredients with which reading furnished their mental cauldron rare and strongly flavoured elements which gave a peculiar pungency to the whole. Nor have they greatly influenced later writers by their mode of writing. It is not as forerunners or successors, as literary innovators or contributors to a tradition, that we read them, but for their intrinsic interest and merit—for the high and singular pleasure, to be obtained from no other writers, which we gain from the strange, matchless, darkly noble quality of their creations.

THE BRONTË FAMILY

A Select Bibliography

(Place of publication London, unless stated otherwise)

Bibliography:

A BRONTË LIBRARY: A Catalogue of Printed Books, Manuscripts, and Autograph Letters by the Members of the Brontë Family, collected by T. J. Wise; privately printed (1929).

CATALOGUE OF THE [Parsonage] MUSEUM AND LIBRARY [at Haworth], THE BRONTË SOCIETY, by J. A. Symington; Haworth (1927)

—a separate Catalogue of the Bonnell Collection in the Haworth Museum was published at Haworth in 1932. See also under *The Shakespeare Head Brontë, Brontë Society Transactions* (Vols I, VI, LIX) and *The Four Brontës*, by L. and E. M. Hanson, 1949.

Collected Works:

POEMS BY CURRER, ELLIS, AND ACTON BELL (1846)

—the unsold sheets were re-issued by Smith Elder in 1848.

THE ORPHANS AND OTHER POEMS, by Charlotte, Emily, and Branwell Brontë; privately printed (1917).

LIFE AND WORKS OF CHARLOTTE BRONTË AND HER SISTERS, 7 vols (1872-3)

—Vol. VII contains the *Life of Charlotte Brontë* by Mrs Gaskell. This edition was republished (1899-1900) as *The Haworth Edition* with Introductions by Mrs Humphry Ward and Notes by C. K. Shorter.

THE WORKS OF CHARLOTTE, EMILY, AND ANNE BRONTË, 12 vols (1893)

—the standard library edition, frequently reprinted.

THE SHAKESPEARE HEAD BRONTË, ed. T. J. Wise and J. A. Symington, 19 vols; Oxford (1931-8)

—the definitive edition to date, though incomplete. Contains the Novels (11 vols), Life and Letters (4 vols), Miscellaneous and Unpublished Writings (2 vols) (Angrian scripts by Charlotte and Branwell), Poems (2 vols), Bibliography.

THE BRONTËS: Life and Letters, by C. K. Shorter, 2 vols (1908)

—the correspondence, here printed for the first time in chronological order, does not include the letters to Mr and Mrs George Smith (printed in *The Haworth Edition*) or those to Monsieur Heger and others (printed in *The Shakespeare Head Brontë*).

THE BRONTË LETTERS, ed. Muriel Spark (1954)
—a selection of 130 letters from the Brontës and other relevant correspondents.

Note: The novels of the Brontë Sisters have been published in The World's Classics, Everyman, Nelson Classics, The Heather Edition, Collins Classics and other popular series. There are also many separate hardcover and paperback editions of individual novels.

REVD PATRICK BRONTË

Separate Works:

COTTAGE POEMS; Halifax (1811). *Poems*

THE RURAL MINSTREL; Halifax (1813). *Poems*

THE COTTAGE IN THE WOOD; Bradford (1815). *Story and Poems*

THE MAID OF KILLARNEY (1818). *Story*

BRONTEANA: Collected Works and Life, ed. J. Horsfall Turner; Bingley (1898).

Critical Studies:

THE FATHER OF THE BRONTËS, by A. B. Hopkins; Baltimore (1958)
—a careful, authentic study.

A MAN OF SORROW: The Life, letters and times of the Rev. Patrick Brontë, 1777-1861, by J. Lock and W. T. Dixon (1965)
—contains every detail at present known about its subject, and new material about the Revd Patrick's parochial work.

CHARLOTTE BRONTË
(*pseud.* Currer Bell)

Separate Works:

JANE EYRE: An Autobiography, edited by Currer Bell, 3 vols (1847). *Novel*
—reprinted 1848 as 'By Currer Bell', with Preface.

SHIRLEY: A Tale, 3 vols (1849). *Novel*

VILLETTE, 3 vols (1853). *Novel*

THE PROFESSOR: A Tale, 2 vols (1857). *Novel*
—reprinted 1860 with *Emma*, a fragment of a Novel, first published in the *Cornhill Magazine*, 1860.

COMPLETE POEMS OF CHARLOTTE BRONTË, ed. C. K. Shorter and collected, with bibliography and notes, by C. W. Hatfield (1923).

THE TWELVE ADVENTURERS AND OTHER STORIES, ed. C. K. Shorter (1925).

THE SPELL: An Extravaganza, ed. G. E. Maclean; Oxford (1931). *Juvenilia*

LEGENDS OF ANGRIA. Compiled by F. E. Ratchford and W. C. de Vane; New Haven (1933). *Juvenilia*

—a number of Charlotte Brontë's poems, stories, and fragments were privately printed in separate editions by C. K. Shorter.

FIVE NOVELETTES: Transcribed from the original manuscripts, ed. W. Gérin (1971)

—comprising novelettes written by Charlotte Brontë in her twenties: *Passing Events; Julia; Mina Laury; Henry Hastings; Caroline Vernon.*

Critical Studies:

LIFE OF CHARLOTTE BRONTË, by E. C. Gaskell, 2 vols (1857)

—the third edition, 1857, of this standard biography was 'revised and corrected', and has since been reprinted many times.

CHARLOTTE BRONTË: A Monograph, by Sir T. W. Reid (1877)

—contains material unknown to Mrs Gaskell.

THE BRONTË STORY: A Reconsideration of Mrs Gaskell's *Life of Charlotte Brontë*, by M. Lane (1953).

THE ACCENTS OF PERSUASION: Charlotte Brontë's novels, by R. B. Martin (1966)

—full-length critical analysis of Charlotte's four novels as works of art.

CHARLOTTE BRONTË: the Evolution of Genius, by W. Gérin; Oxford (1967)

—all the Gérin books are works of solid original research, very fully documented.

CHARLOTTE BRONTË, by A. Pollard (1968).

EMILY JANE BRONTË
(*pseud.* Ellis Bell)

Separate Works:

WUTHERING HEIGHTS: A Novel, 3 vols (1847)

—Anne Brontë's novel *Agnes Grey* occupies the third volume.

WUTHERING HEIGHTS AND AGNES GREY: 'A New Edition revised with A Biographical Notice of the Authors, A Selection from their Literary Remains and a Preface by Currer Bell' (1850). *Novels*

GONDAL POEMS, ed. H. Brown and J. Mott [from the MS in the British Museum]; Oxford (1938). *Juvenilia*

COMPLETE POEMS, ed. C. K. Shorter and arranged and collated, with bibliography and notes, by C. W. Hatfield (1923).

COMPLETE WORKS, ed. C. K. Shorter, with introductory essay by Sir W. R. Nicoll, 2 vols (1910-11).

COMPLETE POEMS, ed. P. Henderson (1951).

GONDAL'S QUEEN: A Novel in verse. Arranged, with introduction and notes, by F. E. Ratchford; Austin, Texas (1955)

—Emily's poems arranged to tell the story of Gondal in chronological order of events.

Critical Studies:

EMILY BRONTË, by A. M. F. Robinson [Mme Duclaux] (1883)
—in the 'Eminent Women' series.

THE STRUCTURE OF 'WUTHERING HEIGHTS', by C. P. S[anger] (1926)
—a useful analytical study.

THE AUTHORSHIP OF 'WUTHERING HEIGHTS', by I. C. Willis (1936)
—analyses the legend of Branwell's participation, giving a long extract from his fragment *And the Weary are at Rest*.

THE BRONTËS' WEB OF CHILDHOOD, by F. E. Ratchford; New York (1941)
—a major work of research into Angrian and Gondal legends.

EMILY BRONTË: Her Life and Work, by M. Spark and D. Stanford (1953)
—contains an attempt to evaluate Emily's works in their own right and not as biographical extensions.

EMILY BRONTË: A Critical and biographical study, by J. Hewish (1969).

EMILY BRONTË: 'WUTHERING HEIGHTS': A Casebook, by M. Allott (1970).

ANNE BRONTË
(*pseud.* Acton Bell)

Separate Works:

AGNES GREY: A Novel (1847)
—first published as Vol III of Emily Brontë's *Wuthering Heights*.

THE TENANT OF WILDFELL HALL, 3 vols (1848). *Novel*
—reprinted with a Preface in 1850.

COMPLETE POEMS, ed. C. K. Shorter, with a bibliographical introduction by C. W. Hatfield (1921).

Critical Studies:

ANNE BRONTË: Her life and writings, by W. T. Hale; Bloomington, Indiana (1929).

ANNE BRONTË, by W. Gérin; Edinburgh (1959).

ANNE BRONTË: Her life and Work, by A. M. Harrison and D. Stanford (1959).

PATRICK BRANWELL BRONTË

Separate Works:

THE ODES OF HORACE—First Book. Translated by Branwell Brontë, ed. J. Drinkwater (1923).

'AND THE WEARY ARE AT REST', ed. J. A. Symington and C. W. Hatfield; privately printed (1924). *Fragment of novel*
—see also *The Shakespeare Head Brontë.*

Critical Studies:

THE BRONTË FAMILY: With special reference to Patrick Branwell Brontë, by F. A. Leyland, 2 vols (1886).

THE INFERNAL WORLD OF BRANWELL BRONTË, by D. du Maurier (1960)
—a biography with special reference to Branwell's states of mind.

BRANWELL BRONTË, by W. Gérin (1961).

Some General Biographical and Critical Studies:

HAWORTH PAST AND PRESENT, by J. Horsfall Turner; Brighouse (1879).

BRONTË SOCIETY TRANSACTIONS; Bradford (1895-)
—contains unpublished fragments, juvenilia, biographical notes, and other articles relating to the Brontës. Selections from the *Transactions* were reprinted in 1947 as *The Brontës Then and Now.*

LES SŒURS BRONTË, by E. Dimnet; Paris (1910)
—the most important foreign study. English translation by L. M. Sill, 1927.

IN THE FOOTSTEPS OF THE BRONTËS, by Mrs E. A. Chadwick (1914)
—the author knew Monsieur Heger's son and one of the Brontë servants.

MRS GASKELL AND HER FRIENDS, by E. S. Haldane (1930)
—includes unpublished letters about Haworth and the Revd P. Brontë.

THE BRONTËS: Their Lives, Friendships, and Correspondence, by T. J. Wise and J. A. Symington, 4 vols; Oxford (1932)
—Vols XII-XV of *The Shakespeare Head Brontë*: the fullest and most authoritative biography.

THE BRONTËS: Their Lives Recorded by Their Contemporaries, compiled with an introduction by E. M. Delafield (1935).

THE CLUE TO THE BRONTËS, by G. E. Harrison (1948)

—contains new information about Methodist factors in Brontë parentage.

THE FOUR BRONTËS: The Lives and Works of Charlotte, Branwell, Emily, and Ann Brontë, by L. and E. M. Hanson (1949)

—contains a full list of biographical and critical studies of the Brontës.

THEIR PROPER SPHERE, by I. S. Ewbank (1966)

—study of the Brontë sisters as early Victorian female novelists.

LE SECRET DES BRONTË, by C. Maurat; Paris (1967)

—translated into English as *The Brontës' Secret*, by M. Meldrum, 1969.

THE BRONTË NOVELS, by W. A. Craik (1968).

HAWORTH AND THE BRONTËS: A Visitor's Guide, by W. R. Mitchell; Clapham, Lancaster (1967).

CRITICS OF CHARLOTTE AND EMILY BRONTË, ed. J. O'Neill (1968).

EMILY AND ANNE BRONTË, by N. Sherry (1969).

THE BRONTËS AND THEIR WORLD, by Phyllis Bentley (1969)

—a useful collection of 140 pictures, with text.

HAWORTH HARVEST: The Lives of the Brontës, by N. Brysson Morrison (1969).

WRITERS AND THEIR WORK

General Surveys:
THE DETECTIVE STORY IN BRITAIN: Julian Symons
THE ENGLISH BIBLE: Donald Coggan
ENGLISH VERSE EPIGRAM: G. Rostrevor Hamilton
ENGLISH HYMNS: A. Pollard
ENGLISH MARITIME WRITING: Hakluyt to Cook: Oliver Warner
THE ENGLISH SHORT STORY I: & II: T. O. Beachcroft
THE ENGLISH SONNET: P. Cruttwell
ENGLISH SERMONS: Arthur Pollard
ENGLISH TRANSLATORS and TRANSLATIONS: J. M. Cohen
ENGLISH TRAVELLERS IN THE NEAR EAST: Robin Fedden
THREE WOMEN DIARISTS: M. Willy

Sixteenth Century and Earlier:
FRANCIS BACON: J. Max Patrick
BEAUMONT & FLETCHER: Ian Fletcher
CHAUCER: Nevill Coghill
GOWER & LYDGATE: Derek Pearsall
RICHARD HOOKER: A. Pollard
THOMAS KYD: Philip Edwards
LANGLAND: Nevill Coghill
LYLY & PEELE: G. K. Hunter
MALORY: M. C. Bradbrook
MARLOWE: Philip Henderson
SIR THOMAS MORE: E. E. Reynolds
RALEGH: Agnes Latham
SIDNEY: Kenneth Muir
SKELTON: Peter Green
SPENSER: Rosemary Freeman
THREE 14TH-CENTURY ENGLISH MYSTICS: Phyllis Hodgson
TWO SCOTS CHAUCERIANS: H. Harvey Wood
WYATT: Sergio Baldi

Seventeenth Century:
SIR THOMAS BROWNE: Peter Green
BUNYAN: Henri Talon
CAVALIER POETS: Robin Skelton
CONGREVE: Bonamy Dobrée
DONNE: F. Kermode
DRYDEN: Bonamy Dobrée
ENGLISH DIARISTS: Evelyn and Pepys: M. Willy
FARQUHAR: A. J. Farmer
JOHN FORD: Clifford Leech
GEORGE HERBERT: T. S. Eliot
HERRICK: John Press
HOBBES: T. E. Jessop
BEN JONSON: J. B. Bamborough

LOCKE: Maurice Cranston
ANDREW MARVELL: John Press
MILTON: E. M. W. Tillyard
RESTORATION COURT POETS: V. de S. Pinto
SHAKESPEARE: C. J. Sisson
CHRONICLES: Clifford Leech
EARLY COMEDIES: Derek Traversi
LATER COMEDIES: G. K. Hunter
FINAL PLAYS: F. Kermode
HISTORIES: L. C. Knights
POEMS: F. T. Prince
PROBLEM PLAYS: Peter Ure
ROMAN PLAYS: T. J. B. Spencer
GREAT TRAGEDIES: Kenneth Muir
THREE METAPHYSICAL POETS: Margaret Willy
WEBSTER: Ian Scott-Kilvert
WYCHERLEY: P. F. Vernon

Eighteenth Century:
BERKELEY: T. E. Jessop
BLAKE: Kathleen Raine
BOSWELL: P. A. W. Collins
BURKE: T. E. Utley
BURNS: David Daiches
WM. COLLINS: Oswald Doughty
COWPER: N. Nicholson
CRABBE: R. L. Brett
DEFOE: J. R. Sutherland
FIELDING: John Butt
GAY: Oliver Warner
GIBBON: C. V. Wedgwood
GOLDSMITH: A. Norman Jeffares
GRAY: R. W. Ketton-Cremer
HUME: Montgomery Belgion
SAMUEL JOHNSON: S. C. Roberts
POPE: Ian Jack
RICHARDSON: R. F. Brissenden
SHERIDAN: W. A. Darlington
CHRISTOPHER SMART: G. Grigson
SMOLLETT: Laurence Brander
STEELE, ADDISON: A. R. Humphreys
STERNE: D. W. Jefferson
SWIFT: J. Middleton Murry
SIR JOHN VANBRUGH: Bernard Harris
HORACE WALPOLE: Hugh Honour

Nineteenth Century:
MATTHEW ARNOLD: Kenneth Allott
JANE AUSTEN: S. Townsend Warner
BAGEHOT: N. St John-Stevas
BRONTË SISTERS: Phyllis Bentley
BROWNING: John Bryson
E. B. BROWNING: Alethea Hayter
SAMUEL BUTLER: G. D. H. Cole
BYRON: Bernard Blackstone

CARLYLE: David Gascoyne
LEWIS CARROLL: Derek Hudson
COLERIDGE: Kathleen Raine
CREEVEY & GREVILLE: J. Richardson
DE QUINCEY: Hugh Sykes Davies
DICKENS: K. J. Fielding
    EARLY NOVELS: T. Blount
    LATER NOVELS: B. Hardy
DISRAELI: Paul Bloomfield
GEORGE ELIOT: Lettice Cooper
FERRIER & GALT: W. M. Parker
FITZGERALD: Joanna Richardson
ELIZABETH GASKELL: Miriam Allott
GISSING: A. C. Ward
THOMAS HARDY: R. A. Scott-James
        and C. Day Lewis
HAZLITT: J. B. Priestley
HOOD: Laurence Brander
G. M. HOPKINS: Geoffrey Grigson
T. H. HUXLEY: William Irvine
KEATS: Edmund Blunden
LAMB: Edmund Blunden
LANDOR: G. Rostrevor Hamilton
EDWARD LEAR: Joanna Richardson
MACAULAY: G. R. Potter
MEREDITH: Phyllis Bartlett
JOHN STUART MILL: M. Cranston
WILLIAM MORRIS: P. Henderson
NEWMAN: J. M. Cameron
PATER: Ian Fletcher
PEACOCK: J. I. M. Stewart
ROSSETTI: Oswald Doughty
CHRISTINA ROSSETTI: G. Battiscombe
RUSKIN: Peter Quennell
SIR WALTER SCOTT: Ian Jack
SHELLEY: G. M. Matthews
SOUTHEY: Geoffrey Carnall
LESLIE STEPHEN: Phyllis Grosskurth
R. L. STEVENSON: G. B. Stern
SWINBURNE: H. J. C. Grierson
TENNYSON: B. C. Southam
THACKERAY: Laurence Brander
FRANCIS THOMPSON: P. Butter
TROLLOPE: Hugh Sykes Davies
OSCAR WILDE: James Laver
WORDSWORTH: Helen Darbishire

Twentieth Century:

CHINUA ACHEBE: A. Ravenscroft
W. H. AUDEN: Richard Hoggart
HILAIRE BELLOC: Renée Haynes
ARNOLD BENNETT: F. Swinnerton
EDMUND BLUNDEN: Alec M. Hardie
ROBERT BRIDGES: J. Sparrow
ROY CAMPBELL: David Wright
JOYCE CARY: Walter Allen
G. K. CHESTERTON: C. Hollis
WINSTON CHURCHILL: John Connell

R. G. COLLINGWOOD: E. W. F. Tomlin
I. COMPTON-BURNETT:
        R. Glynn Grylls
JOSEPH CONRAD: Oliver Warner
WALTER DE LA MARE: K. Hopkins
NORMAN DOUGLAS: Ian Greenlees
LAWRENCE DURRELL: G. S. Fraser
T. S. ELIOT: M. C. Bradbrook
FIRBANK & BETJEMAN: J. Brooke
FORD MADOX FORD: Kenneth Young
E. M. FORSTER: Rex Warner
CHRISTOPHER FRY: Derek Stanford
JOHN GALSWORTHY: R. H. Mottram
WM. GOLDING: Clive Pemberton
ROBERT GRAVES: M. Seymour-Smith
GRAHAM GREENE: Francis Wyndham
L. P. HARTLEY: Paul Bloomfield
A. E. HOUSMAN: Ian Scott-Kilvert
ALDOUS HUXLEY: Jocelyn Brooke
HENRY JAMES: Michael Swan
PAMELA HANSFORD JOHNSON:
        Isabel Quigly
JAMES JOYCE: J. I. M. Stewart
RUDYARD KIPLING: Bonamy Dobrée
D. H. LAWRENCE: Kenneth Young
C. DAY LEWIS: Clifford Dyment
WYNDHAM LEWIS: E. W. F. Tomlin
COMPTON MACKENZIE: K. Young
LOUIS MACNEICE: John Press
KATHERINE MANSFIELD: Ian Gordon
JOHN MASEFIELD: L. A. G. Strong
SOMERSET MAUGHAM: J. Brophy
GEORGE MOORE: A. Norman Jeffares
J. MIDDLETON MURRY: Philip Mairet
SEAN O'CASEY: W. A. Armstrong
GEORGE ORWELL: Tom Hopkinson
JOHN OSBORNE: Simon Trussler
HAROLD PINTER: John Russell Taylor
POETS OF 1939–45 WAR: R. N. Currey
ANTHONY POWELL: Bernard Bergonzi
POWYS BROTHERS: R. C. Churchill
J. B. PRIESTLEY: Ivor Brown
HERBERT READ: Francis Berry
FOUR REALIST NOVELISTS: V. Brome
BERNARD SHAW: A. C. Ward
EDITH SITWELL: John Lehmann
KENNETH SLESSOR: C. Semmler
C. P. SNOW: William Cooper
SYNGE & LADY GREGORY: E. Coxhead
DYLAN THOMAS: G. S. Fraser
G. M. TREVELYAN: J. H. Plumb
WAR POETS: 1914–18: E. Blunden
EVELYN WAUGH: Christopher Hollis
H. G. WELLS: Montgomery Belgion
PATRICK WHITE: R. F. Brissenden
ANGUS WILSON: K. W. Gransden
VIRGINIA WOOLF: B. Blackstone
W. B. YEATS: G. S. Fraser